Poems of Love and Marriage

Poems of Love
and Marriage

John Ciardi

The University of Arkansas Press

Fayetteville   London

1988

Designer: Chiquita Babb
Typeface: Linotron 202 Baskerville
Typesetter: G & S Typesetters, Inc.
Printer: Thomson-Shore, Inc.
Binder: John H. Dekker & Sons, Inc.

The paper used in this publication meets the
minimum requirements of the American National
Standard for Permanence of Paper for Printed
Library Materials z39.48-1984. ∞

Library of Congress Cataloging-in-Publication Data

Ciardi, John, 1916–1986
   Poems of love and marriage.
      1. Love poetry, American.   2. Marriage—Poetry.
I. Title.
PS3505.I27P6   1988   811'.52   88-17229
ISBN 1-55728-053-1 (alk. paper)
ISBN 1-55728-055-X (deluxe : alk. paper)
ISBN 1-55728-054-1 (pbk. : alk. paper)

For Judith

Waiting
Seems to be most of everything.
It keeps growing. It can stretch
past seeing and being and still
be only starting to start.

It ends where you begin.

Contents

Poems of Love and Marriage

In Pity as We Kiss and Lie

Softly wrong, we lie and kiss,
heart to heart and thigh to thigh.
Like man and woman. As if this
were how and who and when and why.

Some two in the time of man
and woman found it sweet
to trade what such half-bodies can
that both be made complete.

Some two in a place that was
hardly right but softly true
found themselves and founded us—
he to her and I to you.

Softly wrong and hardly right,
heart to heart and thigh to thigh,
in each others arms tonight
we lie and kiss and kiss and lie.

If he by her and I by you,
like man and woman, now and then
find each other softly true—
what of how, who, why, and when?

Till hardly wrong, as mercy is—
when and how and who and why—
softly right we lie and kiss
in pity as we kiss and lie.

The Stills and Rapids of Your Nakedness

The stills and rapids of your nakedness
in the bird-started morning mist of sun
spill from my sleep like April's waking rush
into the groundswell and green push of May.

All days tell this, Season and season, this.
This apple to my mind's eye. This new bread.
This well of living water where the bell
of heaven is. This home's door and first kiss.

Darling, to see your eyes when you, too, stir,
turn all their inner weathers to a smile
I write you this: a jargon in the sky
twitters about your sleep; and like a churning

the dawn beats into gold; and, like a field
the wind turns over, all your body lives
its circling blood; and like the first of leaves,
I start from wood to praise you and grow green.

Everytime You Are Sleeping

Everytime you are sleeping and I
am not I like to watch your far
breathing wakefully counting this
and far nights tenderly dark with
thoughts closely and farther yet
nights when you will not be closely
thus thought of in any way nor I

Sometimes the Foundering Fury

Sometimes the foundering fury that directs
the prayer through storm, the sucking mouth;
sometimes a gentleness like a parent sex;
sometimes an aimless tasting mild as broth

or the drugged eye of the invalid; sometimes
a naked arm laid loose along the grass
to the brown-eyed breast and the great terms
of the turning flank printed by root and moss;

sometimes a country in a white bird's eye
coasting the shells of cities in their past,
the roads that stretch to nothing but away,
a horseman wandering in his own dust—

say you were beautiful those years ago,
flush as the honey-blonde who rode the shell
in Sandro Botticelli's studio,
and what we are now, we were then,

and lost, and found again—what shall we wish
to visit from ourselves against that death
but their imagination on our flesh?
There is no other body in all myth.

Returning Home

I want to tell you a
gentlest thing. Like light
to you. Like old faces
being fed a good memory
from inside themselves.
Like eyes that do not
watch but slowly meet
across a room in which
everyone is, and no one
need hurry to what he is
sure of. I want to say
before we run out of
rooms and everyone
that I am slowest,
surest, gentlest, too,
across whatever room
I look at you.

*T*o Judith Asleep

My dear, darkened in sleep, turned from the moon
That riots on curtain-stir with every breeze
Leaping in moths of light across your back . . .
Far off, then soft and sudden as petals shower
Down from wired roses—silently, all at once—
You turn, abandoned and naked, all let down
In ferny streams of sleep and petaled thighs
Rippling into my flesh's buzzing garden.

Far and familiar your body's myth-map lights,
Traveled by moon and dapple. Sagas were curved
Like scimitars to you hips. The raiders' ships
All sailed to your one port. And watchfires burned
Your image on the hills. Sweetly you drown
Male centuries in your chiaroscuro tide
Of breast and breath. And all my memory's shores
You frighten perfectly, washed familiar and far.

Ritual wars have climbed your shadowed flank
Where bravos dreaming of fair women tore
Rock out of rock to have your cities down
In loot of hearths and trophies of desire.
And desert monks have fought your image back
In a hysteria of mad skeletons.
Bravo and monk (the heads and tails of love)
I stand, a spinning coin of wish and dread,

Counting our life, our chairs, our books and walls,
Our clock whose radium eye and insect voice
Owns all our light and shade, and your white shell
Spiraled in moonlight on the bed's white beach;
Thinking, I might press you to my ear
And all your coils fall out in sounds of surf
Washing a mystery sudden as you are
A light on light in light beyond the light.

Child, child, and making legend of my wish
Fastened alive into your naked sprawl—
Stir once to stop my fear and miser's panic
That time shall have you last and legendry
Undress to old bones from its moon brocade.
Yet sleep and keep our prime of time alive
Before that death of legend. My dear of all

Saga and century, sleep in familiar-far.
Time still must tick *this is, I am, we are.*

*T*hree A. M. and Then Five

"Do you like your life?"
said the ghost of God-shadow
one wisp of a night blowing.

"You woke me to ask that?"
I growled through the phlegm of sleep.
"What else would wake you?" it said.

I wallowed in that wind forever,
the sheets a hair shirt,
practice-praying to no address.

Till my wife said, "Please lie still!"
So I went down into the wind
to where I had left the bourbon.

"No one knows me better," I told it.
"What do you think?"
"I may be too good for you," it said.

But it gentled, glowed, at last
whispered, "Go to sleep now."
I went back, the bed warm with her,

the sheets satin.
"Yes," I said to the ghost
yawningly, "Yes. Yes."

*M*orning

A morning of the life there is
in the house beginning again
its clutters in the sun

babbles and sways and tells
time from its sailing cribs. Enter
three pirate energies to murder sleep:

the bed rocks with their boarding:
a fusilade of blather
sweeps the white decks. We're taken!

—Good morning, sweet with chains.
We win all but the fight.
Do as they say—I'll meet you here tonight.

The Stone without Edges Has Not Been Mined

The stone without edges has not been mined,
and the kiss that does not lie has not been joined.
Nothing falls from Heaven but of its weight.
      I love you of my loss.

What day begets the child of no nuisance?
In a tantrum after tenderness, for nothing,
I have slapped the child of our impudence.
      I love you of my shame.

Be old leather. Dry, as a hide in sun
cracks and turns dust and puffs at a touch,
once airborne pastes of life have smeared it.
      I love you of our death.

The bride without escapes has not been kissed,
nor the groom without terrors. Having dared
our own tears and a child's, we have our healing.
      I love you of that health.

That Summer's Shore

On the Island, finding you naked and pearled
in a summer sea, and our daughter naked by you,
at froth with the universe and laughing a splendor
into the huff and sneeze-out of the swell—

finding you there, you two, by that most world
most spoken, saying from time
how we are inhaled and exhaled by a sound
between two water-heaves, I swore

to speak the deeps of the kiss of man and woman,
to say you as you are inside my breath
after the turning apart of arms from their twining,
in the night nest before sleep, yet truer than waking,

warm from your warmth, this man beside this woman,
all man beside all woman, at touch and Adamic.
I speak that nearness in the tongue of prayer,
seeing you distanced by sea that distances all,

yet naked as all touch of human nights
housed in their candle-breath above the huff,
my hand shaped into sleep across your hand
as anything in nature seeks its resting.

So, returning from the Mainland, I found you
there in the sea in your woman nakedness,
and the girl in her girl nakedness, and the sea
silken and long and breathing of our sleep.

In Species, Darling

In species, darling, consider how the whale,
a cousin of a sort, once paddled,
as we did yesterday, in summer shallows,

and then went deep. It did not tire, as we did,
of salt that first braced and then stung.
Something called it out and us back,

each to the thing nearest its happiness
as each finds it. I thank you for my kind
against the belittling sea. In idiom

one says, "I love you." Idiom, however,
is the skin of meaning. At whole body depth
we are tropisms, the way each species has

of turning toward some things and away from others.
I turn to you and tremble to a balance.
Or turn and tip to that beam-breaking sea.

The Deaths They Are,
Those Great Eyes from the Air

The deaths they are, those great eyes from the air
like water-globes hung in their seven lights,
watch at all gardens, shedding dews of grace
when lovers most remember what to do.

Then slags burn mineral rainbows, ruins come caroling
out of their rake-teeth and sag, wrack
spumes far as the last keel's going, and time
shivers a tropic of bells and vibrations

in the blood of beginning again. What other pool
than the moon-flesh of lovers watched from their past
will change a star's reflection to a thought
that justifies the listening of the air?

It is my father drives me from his dust
among my bones' moon-arches, his and his,
and spins the whirlpool on my pole of flesh,
and spines the air with trellises of notes;

until I will your flesh to all their deaths,
and to all mine, and to the lives between,
in such a choir-burst as the season's are
under their dome of winds that stir your hair.

What World It Is the Crocodile May Know

What world it is the crocodile may know
   Gorged in the rotten heavens of his mud,
Or swirling in white water on his cow
   Till every storm is second to his blood.

Or think how vultures out of Nature's mind
   Descend like rancid angels to their chicks
Bearing the carrion mercy on the wind
   From stinking bones to shelves of stinking sticks.

Spill. Spill. These jaws have splendor, these beaks grace.
   It is that world walked on by storms of light
I hold you in to hold my blood in place
   Till angels come to break me in the night.

*I*t Is Spring, Darling

It is Spring, darling, and the five feathers
a-tickle in my wits, those five furry antennae
the spun self spins out to the rayed weathers,
twitch and receive new airs. A slight uncanny
ripple stirs the skin. I learn how far
into the threaded wood the young wolf reaches,
his sense trembling, turning hair by hair
the prescience wound in creatures.

It is Spring, and never again perfectly, but always
again as if the language born of things
spoke itself whole, I take days
as if spoken, light as it brings
great green scripts into view. And since my most
green-spoken and green-written tongue is you,
I speak and read my senses, season-tossed,
to their first rushing Logos ringing through

the morning of the world begun,
the first arriving airs
through which the young wolves run
along the quick, cocked to their dowsing ears
and instant noses. Darling, I am slow
and human and the wood outruns my blood.
I fill with tongues I do not wholly know,
with prowling senses never understood,

tracking my five wits to their deepest den,
where you wait in the first of time again.

*M*en Marry What They Need

Men marry what they need. I marry you,
morning by morning, day by day, night by night,
and every marriage makes this marriage new.

In the broken name of heaven, in the light
that shatters granite, by the spitting shore,
in air that leaps and wobbles like a kite,

I marry you from time and a great door
is shut and stays shut against wind, sea, stone,
sunburst, and heavenfall. And home once more

inside our walls of skin and struts of bone,
man-woman, woman-man, and each the other,
I marry you by all dark and all dawn

and have my laugh at death. Why should I bother
the flies about me? Let them buzz and do.
Men marry their queen, their daughter, or their mother

by hidden names, but that thin buzz whines through:
where reasons are no reason, cause is true.
Men marry what they need. I marry you.

Most like an Arch This Marriage

Most like an arch—an entrance which upholds
and shores the stone-crush up the air like lace.
Mass made idea, and idea held in place.
A lock in time. Inside half-heaven unfolds.

Most like an arch—two weaknesses that lean
into a strength. Two fallings become firm.
Two joined abeyances become a term
naming the fact that teaches fact to mean.

Not quite that? Not much less. World as it is,
what's strong and separate falters. All I do
at piling stone on stone apart from you
is roofless around nothing. Till we kiss

I am no more than upright and unset.
It is by falling in and in we make
the all-bearing point, for one another's sake,
in faultless failing, raised by our own weight.

The Deaths about You When You Stir in Sleep

The deaths about you when you stir in sleep
hasten me toward you. Out of the bitter mouth
that sours the dark, I sigh for what we are
who heave our vines of blood against the air.

Old men have touched their dreaming to their hearts:
that is their age. I touch the moment's dream
and shrink like them into the thing we are
who drag our sleeps behind us like a fear.

Murderers have prayed their victims to escape,
then killed because they stayed. In murdering time
I think of rescues from the thing we are
who cannot slip one midnight from the year.

Scholars have sunk their eyes in penitence
for sins themselves invented. Sick as Faust
I trade with devils, damning what we are
who walk our dreams out on a leaning tower.

Saints on their swollen knees have banged at death:
it opened; they fell still. I bang at life
to knock the walls away from what we are
who raise our deaths about us when we stir.

Lovers unfevering sonnets from their blood
have burned with patience, laboring to make fast
one blood-beat of the bursting thing we are.
I have no time. I love you by despair.

Till on the midnight of the thing we are
the deaths that nod about us when we stir,
wake and become. Once past that fitful hour
our best will be to dream of what we were.

*M*orning: I Know Perfectly How in a Minute You Will Stretch and Smile

As pilots pay attention to the air
    lounging on triggers wired into their ease;
    seeing what they do not see, because their eyes
    are separate cells; hearing what they do not hear,
    because a life is listening in their place;
    and so with their five senses and a sixth
    cocked to their element, free and transfixed,
    slouch as they hurtle, ticking as they laze—

so in the mastered master element
    love is or nothing, silences unheard,
    flickerings unseen, and every balancing
    and tremor of our senses still unsensed,
    joins and enjoins, and, nothing left to chance,
    spins our precisions in us as we nod.

I Was Not Sleeping nor Awake

I was not sleeping nor awake. It was
that hour that beaches from the change of sleep:
a touch first, then a shove, and then the wash
of a tide's leaving. Flotsam, still half deep
in the sucked edge that is half sea, half land,
I lay, still blinded, and put out my hand.

It was my hand awoke me. It reached out
and touched where you should be and you were gone.
I sat up, still half nightmared by some thought
the sea had not washed back, half man again
and half a creature still—and you were there
before your mirror, doing up your hair.

I sat back and, a chuckle in my head
the sea has never heard, thought how a priest
might die and, being certain he was dead,
wake to start heaven, and find himself at rest
on nothing, and unwitnessed to that deep.
—Had I been lying out there in my sleep?

my collar turned? my sermon on my cuff?
and all my service canceled to a truth?
Who knows what sleep connects? I'd had enough
of floating edges and the idiot froth
that bubbles out of sleep. I had arrived
back to some manhood. Back to where we lived.

It was a morning of a house in time.
My hand lay empty, but the fact as full
as any made our room as bright a tomb
as heaven is preached. And if its preachers fall
to nothing, why that's nothing. Not to us.
When I woke, all I thought would be there, was.

Darling

Some have meant only, though curiously,
to believe on evidence. Othello for one,
I suppose he took himself too seriously.
He certainly hadn't much talent for having fun.

No one sets out with intent to become ridiculous.
I used to do push-ups, shower,
read into the lives of the great victorious
and of significant losers. I was sure

something was sure. That there was continuity.
Start with a stone: chip away
whatever is not Apollo—the perpetuity
of Apollo, the locked interplay

of thing and idea—and there you are.
Like Venus from foam, David from a slab
of impossibly cracked Carrara,
soul and its given name even from this flab.

In some sense Commandants
drill time to, this tumescence
of bags and flaps doubling over my pants
is my own doing. But are intentions

nothing? It was done while I wasn't looking,
or looking at something else—at a stone
from which I imagined I was chipping
all that wasn't idea. And down

to gravel too small for anything but bangles,
and too dull for that. I grow, alas,
even tempered. It is ambition jangles.
We have given and taken mercy. Was

a god locked in the ruined stone? I have come
to a continuity of feeling. It is like leaving
a hung jury and coming home
not guilty, not acquitted, not quite believing

there is a possible verdict, but gladly free.
It is true I made a mess of it. I meant
a shape that eluded me.
I could say I half repent

but that's a dramatic luxury beyond my means,
a handkerchief for Othello. Let us
stay bloodless in love, and not in separate scenes
but in one slow thought gentling to forgiveness.

A Love Poem

I have labored for her love.
I could not hide my failure.
Nothing could hide my need.

I believe she is grateful.
I bribed her with dances.
A joy still skims.

It makes no difference
except to me. Except
as she is moved to be kind.

I think she is so moved.
We have taken habit of one another.
I can imagine no other mercy.

It is too late for flying lessons.
The bifocal clouds blur.
I am too heavy to skim

what swims before my eyes.
Darling, forgive me,
I can no longer beat time.

The Something/Nothing Any Love Can Tell

The something/nothing any love can tell,
but no hate hear, what the sad ghost
of a common thought sighs back to from any hell
that memorizes in black what was almost
enough out of time in its kept green—
that, as I may, I wish us.

                         I have seen
no reason to think more can be, nor less.
What is not heaven is a respite we
can be imperfect in, and still let bless
the ghost of what perfections we can see
in some mind's eye, this while a mind and eye
still name the ghost we see our reasons by.

The day long dragbreath of the ghostless trek
through marshes outside love, such as it is,
makes every something nothing. The breakneck
swan dive into a cup at circuses
of angel aerialists gold billboards blare
makes too much of too little. There and there

the trekker ends in quicksand and alone
the diver's act goes wide, once, and no more.
But here, by what can stay of what is gone,
by what may come that never was before—
not till a mercy stirred—what needs and meets
lets start that something nothing still completes.

What does not wish is dead. What does not guess
all wish may come to nothing wastes its breath.
What treks out its numb-numbered singleness
was born distrustful. And what flings its death
from godstarred perches to the watery eye
of a trick universe, so needs to die

it leaves this life still dreaming. I do not
conclude I love you. I awake and find
I do, and then conclude the little/lot
of loving you is something more than mind
can parse a nothing to. And wish us then
your life and mine, till what we are has been.

A Suite for Love

i

How shall I reach you till I have imagined
    my first and last of days, and all days,
    turned and turning, that make and let us
    answer and reach for what we are of time?
    How shall I reach you till I have imagined?

Time sags in the middle. Our nights outrun us.
    All energy and impromptu, the flown children
    of our best, leap, strewing our pauses
    with clatters of their shining ignorance.
    How shall I reach you till I have imagined

earth as it is, world as we are—a sum
    of man and woman reached imagining?
    "I love you," says a tongue too Protestant
    for nights, too Catholic for days.
    And so with all men of this tongueless time

I can say nothing till I have imagined
    by long ways round the saying
    what part of what truth tells us as we are
    who reach, and think to reach. To truth?
    Truths are not spoken whole, nor all at once.

ii

An earth taste in the stay of love is first.
    Begun before itself. As earth was
    whose rains hissed striking centuries long into
    hot original stone cups. A sea starting.
    Millennia of steams to a first horizon

visible, and none to see it—an out-of-time.
    If there is time in the kiln, firing and cooling,
    the locked shapes do not keep
    it, but themselves. Shapes are
    not time but things. There is this earth

come from its kiln timeless, and a bird called
    through late fern-eras like a mountain-tide
    coming and going. Called: "There is this earth
    of shapes and shadowings. There is this earth,
    and who will think of it?" Till a man thought it.

It is to think his earth again as he
    in the arms of saber-tooth and woman learned
    and learned to stay his death, that I imagine
    what shapes out of what kiln have told
    the praising man his tongues, their first of birdsong.

iii

"There is this earth: what shall you think of it?"
      the bird sings his first dawn again from sleep's end;
      a sky leap into day. If that were all!
      Ah, if it were and every bird-sung hay
      a heaven of bounced angels!

If that were all! To hear the first-told name
      rung out of morning lungs and walk feasted
      on sunburst dewdeeps—
      taken and held by airy abundances
      and armored against time by time!

I wake, and find you in the risen bird's
      outpouring of the darks that store his song
      for the washed apple-harvests of the light.
      And ah, if that were all! If starting
      were all there were of love!

iv

Time sags in the middle. Worlds outrun us.
    Are worlds true? True as any. I have killed
    airily over unknown towns to reach you,
    setting my torch to the world for the world's
    saying. May those deaths be.

I chose them, or there is no choice. There is—
    this world and what shall lovers think of it
    who think love is what chooses? There is this world
    and once inside it, burning, true, I chose—
    wholly as I choose love now—death.

Forgive me if you must, but I will be
    forgiven only for what I am, who am
    choiceless as any, waiting as I may
    for a life to happen to me. As time sags.
    Dreaming to reach you from a first-named need.

One strictness does for all, and love may say it.

V

One strictness does for all. As fat priests know
    how much they eat of what they do not marry,
    and still give up their starved souls to the host,
    I know what food it is that lets me be

part of truth so strictly told it does
    to bring one dove down in the name of love.
    Come to your blowsy darling with the rose
    between his teeth, my love, and let him move

the one stone he can loosen with a prayer:
    to live in the world and be what a man is
    against his death, and nearest to your sleep.
    A tribesman of your body in his night.

vi

My ten red fingers which are each a boy
    close hot as rum. Whatever chucks a rump
    I praise a-cackle in the bounce of whee!

A god who laughs made wine. Let my boys work
    their shaggy time through mosses of the rose.
    I dance Frère Hèrcule's stick flung through the tree,

Rustico slugging the devil to pink Hell,
    Cunnegonde's jewel box. All that shakes a leg
    toward godsent Wives of Bath by Millers told

I raise a hoop for. If Pacelli can,
    or Chaplain Ike, or Papa Poppycock,
    tell them to tell God that I like His hay!

vii

Then, dead and drawn, a quiver at your hip,
  I am the solved man, regal and at ease
  with all my species answered in your arms
  and all my tribes in order in their caves
  and all my names in place inside themselves.

The strictness is to be. To let our lives
  out of our lives, and answer as they come
  like dancers to the music, keeping whole
  by changing when it changes. Or unchanged
  but being one to one another's answers

in every motion outward of the sound.
  I study toward perfection what I know
  in perfect place already: that you are
  what every reaching reaches. And returns.
  Praising and praised, and all made visible.

The Aging Lovers

Why would they want one another,
those two old crocks of habit
up heavy from the stale bed?

Because we are not visible where we dance,
though a word none hears can call us
to the persuasion of kindness, and there sing.